The Lookout Man

PHOENIX POETS

STUART DISCHELL

The Lookout Man

THE UNIVERSITY OF CHICAGO PRESS
Chicago and London

The University of Chicago Press, Chicago 60637
The University of Chicago Press, Ltd., London

Published 2022
Printed in the United States of America

31 30 29 28 27 26 25 24 23 22 1 2 3 4 5

ISBN-13: 978-0-226-81783-5 (paper)
ISBN-13: 978-0-226-81784-2 (e-book)
DOI: https://doi.org/10.7208/chicago/9780226817842.001.0001

Library of Congress Cataloging-in-Publication Data

Names: Dischell, Stuart, author.
Title: The lookout man / Stuart Dischell.
Other titles: Phoenix poets.
Description: Chicago : The University of Chicago, [2022] | Series: Phoenix poets
Identifiers: LCCN 2021034803 | ISBN 9780226817835 (paperback) | ISBN 9780226817842 (ebook)
Subjects: LCGFT: Poetry.
Classification: LCC PS3554.I827 L66 2022 | DDC 811/.54—dc23
LC record available at https://lccn.loc.gov/2021034803

∞ This paper meets the requirements of ANSI/NISO Z39.48-1992 (Permanence of Paper).

for TERRY KENNEDY

Look out, lookout man.

CONTENTS

Acknowledgments xi

ONE

Lines of the Prodigal *3*
The Foreigner *5*
Inside the Statue *6*
Coda (Broken, He Saw Himself at Last) *10*
Lines about Ships at Sea *11*
Lines about Mountains *13*
Lines about Rivers, Then the Sea *14*
Lines about the Snow *16*
Lines about the Wind *17*
Lines above the Tree Line *19*
Lines of Evolutionary Progress *20*
Lines at the End of the Year *21*

TWO

The Work Zone *25*
Taint *28*
Lines in the Outage *29*
The Arcade, 1962 *30*
White Horse Pike *31*
Action in the Pacific *33*
Lines about Emptiness *34*
Time Was the Rider *35*
Lines of the Elderly Orphan *36*
Lines along the Shore *37*

The Last Days on Ocean Lane *38*
Meeting My Parents for a Weekend in New York, 1988 *39*
Lines on the Invention of Shoes *41*
Lines in the Backyard *42*
Lines about Her *43*
For Hubert Desmarest *44*
For Oksana Shachko *46*

THREE

The Streets of the Capital *51*
Lines on a Train to the Alps *53*
Cities of the Blue Coast *54*
In a Corner of the Sky *55*
Lines in Regard to a Morning Swim *56*
The Measurement of Words *58*
Lines of the Mirage *59*
After the Exhibition *60*
The Enchanted Bells *61*
Stormy Tuesdays *63*
Window Peeping into the Garden of Eden *64*
Lines along a Wild Place *65*

Notes, Elegiac 67

ACKNOWLEDGMENTS

Some of these poems appeared in the following periodicals, sometimes as different versions or under different titles:

Agni: "Lines along the Shore"
Alaska Quarterly Review: "Taint" and "The Last Days on Ocean Lane"
Birmingham Poetry Review: "After the Exhibition" and "The Streets of the Capital"
Envelope: "Lines of the Elderly Orphan"
Five Points: "White Horse Pike" and "Action in the Pacific"
Kenyon Review: "Lines about Mountains," "Lines about Rivers, Then the Sea," and "Lines along a Wild Place"
Literary Imagination: "Lines above the Tree Line"
On the Seawall: "Lines about the Wind" and "The Enchanted Bells"
Southeast Review: "Time Was the Rider"
South Florida Poetry Journal: "Lines in Regard to a Morning Swim" and "The Work Zone"
storySouth: "Lines about Her," "Lines in the Backyard," and "Stormy Tuesdays"

Several poems also appeared in the chapbook *Standing on Z* (Greensboro, NC: Unicorn Press, 2016): "The Arcade, 1962" (as "Song of the Arcade"), "Lines about Emptiness" (as "A Song of Emptiness"), "Lines on the Invention of Shoes" (as "On the Invention of Shoes"), "Cities of the Blue Coast," and "In a Corner of the Sky."

One

LINES OF THE PRODIGAL

I go back
To the street
I grew up on

To see if
The house I
Grew up in

Still stands,
But new people
Tore down

Our cottage
By the cold green
Sea and built

Themselves something
Large like a huge
Coconut cake

On a tiny
Dessert plate—
Not at all like

Our house that fit
Just right. My picture
Window faced

The sea where
The sun rose,
And I was the son

In a gold-painted
Room now gone.
No one sought

My advice or
Permission.
They would not

Have found me
If they tried
To ask whether

They could alter
This crucial evidence
Of my past for

Eternity.
I knew when I woke
The paint that lit

My room was not
Real gold.
I could say

I once was
A happy boy
Inside but won't.

THE FOREIGNER

It is snowing in a city where it almost always snows.
Under the arcades, some distant version of myself,
My grandfather, broke but dressed in a modern suit,
In a hat and long coat, holds an umbrella—
A man of the early twentieth century, he has not yet learned
To smile for pictures. He asks in your language if he might
Have one of your cigarettes, and you give him two.

He wants to place the extra one you gave him
In the silver case in his pocket I have kept safe.
But for now, you take a cigarette yourself,
And he lights it for you with a match he has
Kept dry in his long coat pocket. Neither of you
Wants to step out again into the snow. He thanks you
Once more, and it makes you feel good about yourself
Even if you have done terrible things to others that day.

INSIDE THE STATUE

Through the heel and ankle
I enter from the right
The way one enters
A cathedral.

Climbing the narrow stairs,
I feel the pressure in my own shins.
Ascending the tibia to the femur,
Those ahead
Rest on the landing at the knee.
From there I begin
Spiraling to the buckle where
The up and down flights meet
Just below the navel.

Someone has opened a tavern here.
A bald owner brews coffee and pours the drinks,
And two pale daughters serve them on trays.
They are the color white
People get when living in a mine,
But they are not in a mine.
Fluorescent tubes light them.
I ask for water, and they point at bottled water
In the cooler. They are without speech.
The statue is wired for electricity,
But there is no plumbing inside the statue.

A sign in the foyer explains all this
Where a sleepy docent balances awake
Before a model of the statue.

My mind is everywhere.
I recollect the windy streets
Of the capital where I had been
Walking past the embassies just yesterday.
The leaves ran ahead of us.
My dog was ready to follow.
Did I say it was a big dog?
It dragged me by the leash into the park
Where the leaves assembled on the lawn,
Crisp as you would expect in this season,
Underfoot in all directions.
I remember passing through the gates.

I am in the torso
Near the seventh rib,
Taking the zigzag flights underfoot
Through the great cavity
Of chest where the ribs
Like sideways flying buttresses
Suggest the inside of a whale's mouth,
As I ascend to the clavicle,
Then rung by rung up a ladder
Through the long, noble throat
To the wind-swept observation
Deck where I gaze through the eyes
Open to the elements
Above the buildings and treetops.

Pine or cedar mean nothing to the statue.
Gold or rust, it's all the same.
The statue cares nothing for the line
Outside the ticket counter or the women
Waiting on the benches below
For their children to come down
Or the boy selling souvenirs of the statue
Displayed on a table by the left foot.

Before climbing the statue,
I was a citizen like anyone.
Everything was large to me.
Then the wheel of the years
Rode me to this moment.
I should have seen it but I looked elsewhere.
There are smaller statues in the world.
You think you are in armor;
Some when you enter you cannot move at all.

I drop a coin in the scenic viewer.
Men idle outside a liquor store.
Couples walk a path along the river.
Smoke rises from the chimney pots
Of the tile-roofed houses.
The uniformed driver with her empty bus
Checks her tires with a gauge she took
From her shirt pocket. The letter carrier
In his truck reads a magazine.
The merchant sailors on the vessels watch
The dockworkers warehouse the cargo.

The statue does not care about deeds or commerce.
The statue does not see the lives in progress.
If somebody harmed you, the statue would do nothing.
The statue looks through and over and beyond.
The statue is not aware some call it "The Statue"
Or that its image is well known.

I listen through the wire mesh of each ear
While the statue hears nothing.
The wind blows through its hollow brain.
Even pigeons do not roost in its folds.
To stand below the brow of the statue and see out
Its eyes is to understand what is meant by distance
And be embarrassed by all personal thoughts.
The statue has no self, therefore, no self-pity.
If I have a name, I cannot remember it now.

CODA (BROKEN, HE SAW HIMSELF AT LAST)

The Colossus, tallest wonder
Of the ancient world,
Measured thirty-some meters
Tall over the entry to the harbor
Of Rhodes with both feet on a marble plinth;
Yet in more popular versions he stood
Straddling the harbor. Titan-God Helios:
Bronze guardian of Rhodes for fifty-four years
Until he bowed at the shock and broke
At his knees in an earthquake.
Nine hundred camels bore his pieces away.

LINES ABOUT SHIPS AT SEA

People who live inland forget about ships at sea—

Their massive smokestacks and tall decks,
Light towers, ramps, and nimble cranes,
Bridges, conning towers, and the high keels
Terrifying on the open sea to behold—
The stinky ones carting trash, the tuna-
Canning factories afloat, Japanese whalers
With their eternal bad karma, battleships,
Aircraft carriers, transports, trawlers
Freighters, barges, container vessels,
And supertankers carrying LNG.

Semi-illuminated, the ocean liners wait
At dawn outside the port for the armada
Of tugboats. Down the gangplank goes
The procession of passengers and crew.
The captain has a pleasant smile and keeps
His hand locked in a permanent wave,
Like Admiral Byrd frozen at the Pole.
On other piers, stevedores and forklift
Operators transfer the cargo to the acres
Of metal warehouses beside the gas farm.

Picture the ancient crafts adrift in the mind—
Caravels and square-riggers, argosies, barks

And brigantines. Windjammers, schooners,
Clippers, and galleons. And the vile slavers
And rumrunners. Pirates still board craft
In the Persian Gulf and off the Horn of Africa—
But it's oil they are after, not gold—yet
The odd yacht is sometimes found renamed and painted,
The fate of its owners guessed at with throat-crossing gestures.

People who live inland forget about ships at sea.
The storms on the prairie only slow the interstates.

Sometimes in the night one hears the whistle of a train,
But it's nothing like the horn of a ship in the fog at sea.

LINES ABOUT MOUNTAINS

I just learned that mountains kill
More people climbing down them
Than making their brave ascent
And that some have the oldest
Rocks on the earth. Small wonder
They crumble into avalanche,
Having weathered eons to fall.
Mountains must get tired
With so many people climbing
Them and bored with the endless
Boot prints of alpinists in bright garb,
The flagpoles jammed into crags,
Piton, and foothold, the kick
Of the crampon. Metal ladders
Across crevasses. More climbers
Die each summer on Mont Blanc
Than all the Himalayas, its summit
Not as perilous but more frequented
Than Everest or K2. I conclude
The nearer mountain is far
More dangerous than the distant one,
Just as we are more likely to be killed
By the hands of someone we know.

LINES ABOUT RIVERS, THEN THE SEA

I don't like to swim in rivers.
Their lengths and bends trouble me.

If my chest touched against
Riverweeds, I would panic.

No. I don't like to swim in rivers,
But I admire them for being relentless—

Even blind rivers buried under cities
Or rivers that run just a few days a year.

Some rivers create borders between states and nations.
Some rivers stray from their courses

Or are dammed from flowing to neighbors.
I very much like the word *estuary*

And the thought of boats at low tide there,
And I appreciate how a river divides

Pest from Buda, Minneapolis from St. Paul,
Or the banks someone decided were Left and Right.

A current is like a river in the sea.
When I was small, I lived along the beach.

When I got caught in a riptide,
A passing wave brought me home.

LINES ABOUT THE SNOW

The first snow fell before the first word.
No name could be given for it or rain

Or wind or fields with their winter colors,
No name for cold or clouds or sun

Or even the sky. But snow was different.
Once it fell, it appeared to stay forever,

And the nameless world was cold
For a long time, until the melting

Brought the creatures from deep
In caves out into the light.

Once silent, I feared them,
Then screamed the first word.

LINES ABOUT THE WIND

All fuss and bluster, the wind is busy.
It has a long way to go

Across the wide seas in one long breath,
Clearing its throat down the avenues of commerce.

The wind is master of the clouds,
Sends scraps and dust along the highways.

The wind can be fresh, and the wind can be ill.
Everyone has mixed feelings about the wind—

The sirocco, the Santa Ana, and the mistral
(Which sounds like mistress and minstrel)

All make you crazy. You can blame the wind
When you hate your job or beat your kids—

Go off with your colleague for a dirty weekend.
But no one likes it when the wind quits

And stops the chimes in the park
And stalls the sailboats in the public fountains

And the blades cease spinning on the prairie
And gutter leaves halt running toward erosion

And no breeze lifts the horse's tail
Or dries the sweat on a baby's neck.

The letter carrier left his little truck open.
The wind is blowing away my debts.

LINES ABOVE THE TREE LINE

With the melting of the glaciers,
More bodies are being discovered
Of lost hikers, missing alpine
Mountaineers, and even farmers
Who disappeared with nary a yodel
Heard from the bottom of a crevasse
Or the growls of the avalanche tumble.

It must be weird to meet your parents
Fifty years after they left the house
Still wearing the clothes of peasants
With homemade boots and knitted coats
They wore before they disappeared
To tend the cows in the lower pasture
And left you to raise the younger children.

"The rocks are falling and I have no helmet!"
Said Helmut who spoke all the languages
Of Switzerland and English too, who read
Joyce and Beckett and enjoyed the pun
Of his last conscious moment on the rope.
His climbing partner cut him loose after
A night, making sure he was really dead.

LINES OF EVOLUTIONARY PROGRESS

Creatures of the earth,
We gazed upon the sky.

We straightened up and grew taller.
No more thistles in the palm or knuckles

In the dirt. We liked the taste of meat,
And it made our brains and bodies strong.

Some of us trapped the herds in canyons,
Some of us ran them off the cliffs,

Some of us drew their deeds in caves
And lit our walls with rendered fat.

I don't want to stand up. I want to lie
Here in a lawn chair and pretend

I am at the Tahiti Bar in St. Tropez
Where rich people go naked in the sunshine.

LINES AT THE END OF THE YEAR

No pet ever liked to see me pack—
No child for that matter either.

When my parents went out, I feared
They would never come back

From holidays taken without me.
Now they will never come back.

I have not seen a robin that does not like
To drink from a puddle in December

And splash and clean under its wings
When it thinks no one is looking.

Never knew. Never thought. Always said.
I am the Narcissus of the draining sink.

When my door slams, each leaf in the yard looks back.
Where did I go in such a hurry?

Two

THE WORK ZONE

Between cities,
Yellow Caterpillars
And guys in orange
Slickers work
The earth in the rain
While Gus and Dave,
Half a mile apart,
Each hold the opposite
Side of a sign
On a pole that says
STOP and SLOW.
Huge concrete
Pipes are being
Lowered into the ditch
Dug deep in order
To run the next flood-
Water away from
The shopping center.
Some drivers worry
If there's an accident,
They will be late
For doctor's appointments
At the medical plaza.
And others listening
To grim news think
Of a mass grave ahead

So large it requires
Bulldozers to load
The corpses. Stalled,
Most people just stare
At their phone screens,
Searching for alternate
Routes or deleting
Photos or messages
Archived too long;
No one is patient
In the work zone.
One person looks up
To see beer cans
And diapers scattered,
Wildflowers in patches
Along the shoulder,
And what could possibly
Be a deer's hind leg
Once on its way
To the pond in the thickets
Where apartments are rising
On newly made streets.
Sally, an old
Quarter horse
In a fenced pasture
By the gas station,
Watches the drivers
With Phil the goat.
Near the cemetery,
Comfort for mourners
In fast food. A couple

Holds hands by a grave.
Are they getting married?
Mysterious things
Happen in places
Without zoning.
Honk if you love ugly.

TAINT

A taste in the mouth from tinned meat, maybe,
Or some mold in the bread, or an old tomato
That has you smack your lips, but not for savor,
And make a face your dining partner remarks
Upon that makes you unpleasant company.
Something is wrong. Something is tainted.
If you could, you would sniff it in public.
Instead you partake of what you can, believing
You can eat around it. That thing that tasted
A little wrong at first has plans to get you sick—
If not now, you think, in thirty years when
The microbes have taken over your blood.
You can feel this happening already,
But you do not wish to spoil this moment
With your date already looking at their phone
And the server approaching with kind banter.

LINES IN THE OUTAGE

I am angry tonight because another friend died
And my mother and father are dead

And my girlfriend told me I was old and broke
Up with me and a yellow pine in the storm fell

On my roof and the power is out and it continues
To rain and I can't help thinking about rain and sex

And rain and my impending poverty in old age
And the roads blocked with utility trucks

But there's nowhere to go, just the desire
To be taken someplace, to go outside,

Get in a taxi to some past joy, fleeting
Even in back of a cop car or ambulance.

Wait. There is knocking downstairs. Neighbors
With flashlights and loud voices.

THE ARCADE, 1962

Lucky sits on a stool up front making change.
He's into the short con, so count your coins,
And if you break a ten, forget about it—
Sawbucks have a way of becoming fins,
Even with one arm and arthritic fingers,

And don't suppose you will win the great
Stuffed bear, prized by lovers and children.
He can make your pinball game tilt
Just by walking by. Each day he wears
The same striped suit and fedora.

He keeps the bathroom doors locked,
So you have to bother him for the key.
He sleeps in the back room on a cot.
You don't ever have to ask him to show
The scar he got on the beach at Anzio.

WHITE HORSE PIKE

He stayed at an old motel.
The gravel parking lot ended
At the marsh behind it.
The room was 137.
The ice machine
In the passageway
Beside it leaked
And turned a thin line
Of water into a rusty scribble
Just outside the threshold.
Inside, matching nightstands
And an old-style phone
With buttons. He picked it up.
No dial tone sang back.

But if anyone who ever
Knew him well enough not
To take his collect call
Would answer it anyway,
He would faithfully report
Room 137 remains
Wholly un-renovated, re-
tains plywood dressers,
A sofa with a woven fabric
That hides hideous stains,
A rug that leaves dirty heel prints
On the wet bathroom floor.

He could speak of the misery
Of the shower, the underside
Of the toilet seat, and the heating
Unit that pulled in the smoke
From the cigarettes of last summer
When other guests stood outside
Filling their coolers.

He could tell all he knew of random
Motor Lodges he has stayed in
On highways that had names,
Not numbers: the paintings of sunsets
Warming their cinderblock walls,
The stuffed laundry sacks
Of derelict beds, the sheets
Without cotton, the sinks
That do not drain,
The empty swimming pools
And shut-down coffee shops.

The desk clerk must have
A sense of humor to call
People guests in these rooms.
The remote control
Requires a cash deposit,
And the vended candy
At the front desk is sold
Beyond expiration.

ACTION IN THE PACIFIC

You can see by the sleeves
That his cuffs are worn
From too many pressings,
His effort to appear respectable
Even in his yellowed tee shirt,
Ironing in a rooming house
Near the navy yard in Philly—
An image of a heart and a blurred
Word on his forearm
From a time when only sailors
Sported tattoos, having earned them
In battle or travel—but he was far
From open water, the broken ship,
The flaming oil he dove into
That clung to his face and neck
Like the jellyfish that once got him
Bodysurfing in the waves
Off Brigantine
When he was still a person
Who went out in sunlight.

LINES ABOUT EMPTINESS

I like the lake at dawn
When the wind is still.

I like snowfields without footprints
And muddy farm rows with no ruts.

I like a newly paved road
When the asphalt is drying

And the paving trucks are gone
And the lines have not been painted.

I like round cakes uncut
Without candles or names.

Lucky for me that's what I've got,
The table cleared after writing.

TIME WAS THE RIDER

When the numerals
        On its face
Were lost to me
        As well as its hands,
I cursed the days
        And months I could
No longer see
        (Or change beneath
Its crystal with its crown)
        And the time left
I could have repaired
        Its worn buckle
Or clasped the strap
        Torn from my wrist
Like the broken cinch
        Of a miniature saddle,
Small enough to lose
        In the back of a taxi
Or the sheets of a hotel
        While I was traveling.

And you said I held on too tight.

LINES OF THE ELDERLY ORPHAN

Like picking at a flower,
Few petals are left—

Or let me put it another way,
Pal—it's like unwrapping

A mummy to find nothing
Inside, an empty room,

A chamber where you lived
In the days before you left,

Where the names your father called
Hang in the air forever,

Family seated, waiting for dinner,
Baked apples steaming on the counter.

It is very late now, well past supper.
Your father died long ago and then the others.

And all the dogs you knew that ever counted.
Their urns line the breakfront shelf.

LINES ALONG THE SHORE

The blue cabanas bleached to that pastel
Only the apprehender of dawn could achieve,

The feel underfoot rough on the bare insole
Of the novice shore walker.

Shells and coral comprise the sand—
And the sea is flat, flat, flat at low tide,

Broken by the smallest and most infrequent
Of waves and the vagrant curl

Of a swimmer's arm, like an arched
Eyebrow drawn like a fleck on the water.

Between the jetty's boulders, sand crabs
Await the devouring gulls.

The first of fishermen, attentive to bait,
Casts lines that believe in the future.

THE LAST DAYS ON OCEAN LANE

The accordion panels of the hurricane
        Shutters unfold a screechy music
So loud I can hear it for the first
        Time reverberating in its
Rusted and sea-salted glory in the otherwise
        Quiet chasm between condos
Out of season, and I believe how in all
        Worthwhile improvisations
Some sections give themselves freely,
        While others require more
Effort of the artist,
        In this case shod foot
And shoulder, where the steel
        Rods have caught along the rails.
Finally loose, the metal slips once more
        Into its position,
And in the moment I close this curtain
        On the sunlight and the ocean,
On cue through the doorway
        My mother in Chanel,
Dark glasses, and pearls steps into the hallway,
        Purse in hand,
        Ready.

MEETING MY PARENTS FOR A WEEKEND IN NEW YORK, 1988

My father drowned in this water,
My mother said, holding a glass
Filled from the tap, meaning
It ran through the pipes
All the way from the reservoir
Where he was pulled under
Receding waters
After hunting wild parakeets
With her brothers.

The cloudy water
Took a long time
To clear in her hand.
She stared into the glass
As if through the windows
Of public institutions
Where she stood in lines
With her mother
Before the New Deal,
When the neighbors
Made a rent party
To hold off their eviction.

After the bubbles
In the cold water settled,
She took a deep drink

And left a smudge
Of lipstick on the rim,
And I by the window
Looked away at
The horses in the park,
Declining the rest
Of the glass she offered
While my father out of habit
Checked the mattresses for bedbugs.

LINES ON THE INVENTION OF SHOES

I would like to shake the hand of the first person
Who shod the foot for protection against stones
And barbs, the snow, the heat of the ground, etc.

*

I think of the sandals of the legions and of the later importance of cobblers
When walking was the major form of transportation and of the feet
Of thousands of pilgrims along the trails to Compostela.

*

And of our friend's shelf along the wall just above the floor
Where he kept the ones he favored. He was a manly person,
And they were oxfords and brogues and boots.

*

I walked around the city many times but found not
But what I sought among the processions.
What good fortune it is to live in an age of great shoes.

*

Innovators of sole and insole, lace and eyelet,
Vamp and upper, welt and medial, throat and tongue,
My mother feather-dusted the living room in high heels!

LINES IN THE BACKYARD

Have you seen the lights in the windows of the trees?
No one is at home there unless you count what's wild.

Do you know the names of everyone asleep in your leaves?
I am not just talking about genus and species.

It's hard work keeping up with the new ones
Or those passing through the yard for the night.

Once I saw an owl perched on a low-limbed tree.
I never did get its name because it took off soon.

Jake the vole rode its talons to the stars.
He never came back, but a new Jake lives here now.

LINES ABOUT HER

Animals stand at her door sometimes
For the charity of her hand upon their coat,

Not only for the kibble she offers
And fresh water. The birdfeeders

In her yard get filled to the brim, and she never
Minds if the squirrels take a share too.

When it rains, she says it's very good
Because the trees need washing.

And I know what she means, especially in May
When the pollen dusts the leaves.

In the evenings she gets pretty tipsy
When she drinks from a bottle of jug wine,

Says the fact she's had so many lovers
(And I look at her and think about it)

When she was younger is why she needs no one now
Or again. "So, don't even think about it," she says.

FOR HUBERT DESMAREST

(1961–2017)

Not all men who wear red pants could get away
With saying the things he said and not get punched.

Once we nearly hit each other, but we shoved instead,
And I said, "Fait pas chier," *don't make shit*, and he told me,
"Don't even try to speak a little French with me,

You have no past or future tense," and poked a finger
In my chest, and Dominique told us to stop, and Chantal
Locked the door to the bar, and no one could believe
My behavior because they thought I was reasonable.

What a mistake.
I had the worst headache for forever
And woke at dawn to walk the periphery
Of the city for twenty-four kilometers for an article I was writing,
And I didn't contact him till months later,

And we never spoke of our quarrel.
What it was about I cannot recall,
But something I did earlier offended his manners.

We were people who believed grown men
Should wear sports jackets in the evening in a big city
And never sandals on Saturday nights.
We were divorced and missed our dead fathers.

I should have given him air kisses or real ones
On both sides of his unshaven face, but he spared me
That custom. My good friend, the most French Frenchman
I ever knew—we shook hands like Americans.

FOR OKSANA SHACHKO

(1987-2018)

I am Oksana Shachko, yet
I cannot be her because I am not
A young Ukrainian
Woman stripped to the waist
With English words written
In paint across my breasts,
Showing the populace what
It otherwise wants to see
Looking down a girl's blouse
Or on pornographic screens.

I wish I were Oksana Shachko because
In this life I did not mean to
Fit the body of a man,
Wearing a towel around his middle,
Shaving after a long shower,
Living on a wooded lot in NC,
No longer able to contain himself
In the boredom that surrounds his skin.

But never did I want to be a nun
Or learn to paint icons, or
Protest on the roofs of public
Monuments or occupy cathedrals,
Calling out corrupt leaders
Of church and state, or be kidnapped

By government agents who covered
Me in motor oil in the forest
And tried to light me on fire.

But I am nonetheless Oksana
Shachko, her naked body the instrument
Of social justice. In underpants
And a crown of thorns, eyes
Gazing upward, she
Reconstructed Jesus,
Inserting her own figure
Amid the holy iconography.
I AM FREE she drew
Across the canvas of her skin.

I am Oksana Shachko
But cannot pretend I am half my age
Or stand at an easel and know that even
In the dark to a blind person I am not
A good likeness of a woman,
Yet I wanted to speak not just
From myself but my selves.
I wanted to say something
About July 23, 2018, when Oksana
Shachko hanged herself in her apartment.
I had just left the city the day it happened,
And her voice caught in my throat.

Three

THE STREETS OF THE CAPITAL

They met him in a café just outside
The gates of the walled city,
Where he overheard the couple having
Trouble speaking to the waitress when
They asked for their check and directions
To a church he knew in the heart of the old
District that was restored after the war.

He must have been someone important once.
His suit would have been vintage
If a younger person had worn it. His red tie
Was frayed where it was knotted. The old
Waitress was deferential when he rose
From the table and took the map from
Their hands and offered to help them
Find the church they were looking for.
This was long ago, you see, but not so
Long ago, before people held devices
With voices that told them where to turn.

He showed them they were reading the map wrong.
These things happen when you have no compass
Or range of mountains or body of water to guide the direction.
Once people on foot found their way through dense forests
And across mountains by following the stars . . .

He told the couple he would be glad to guide the way.
It was not far from something he wanted to see.
He left extra coins in the saucer on his table.

As they passed through the city gate, now a slow-
Moving street, he said, "We are walking
Across history" and told them of the entries
Of kings and the nearby defenestration of certain
Members of the clergy, bloodlettings
At nearly every corner or intersection.
It was that way with famous cities,
Like museums, too much to know, too much
To take in, a study of meaningful glances
At indistinguishable stones and passageways.
It was like that with everything, everyone.
It was like going to college. That's why people quit.

Then he led them down a side street—
The sole block of empty structures—
An otherwise cleared area, the city was
Changing to show visitors like themselves
The disappeared would not be forgotten.
Plaques were written in preparation.
Wind blew through the broken windows
And brickwork of the facades—the planks
On the scaffolds lay imperturbable.
"I was born there," he said, pointing
Toward the lot behind the buildings
Where nothing stood. He led
Them back to the main street then
And the place named for the saint they sought.

LINES ON A TRAIN TO THE ALPS

Outwitted again by the machinery of life,
It did not occur to me I would be seated

Backward on the train where I would watch
Blurred cities recede, how on this day

I would travel in the wrong direction,
Forever departing, saying farewell to

High-rise and spire,
Smokestack and tower.

The farmers in the field already
Had done their work when I passed.

All was conclusion, nothing beginning
Until I arrived in Lausanne and turned around.

CITIES OF THE BLUE COAST

He was writing a book called *Cities of the Blue Coast*,
A work in which he was both protagonist and narrator,
"A pilgrim to the past and a stranger to the present,"
He told his brother the autumn before he disappeared
Doing what he had meant to do half a life ago—
Get his legs strong again climbing the high paths
Across the cols and passes to the mountain villages,
Then acreages of lavender and rosemary underfoot
And lemon trees just above the eye. He would trek the
Fragrant hillsides and valleys, up the old crags to a tavern
Where the fish was as fresh as a dead thing could be
And eat the harvest of this world that still had flavor.

IN A CORNER OF THE SKY

Too bad the sun could not stay longer on the water
Or the tide retreat further down the neckline of the beach
Where the sea hides from sight its prettiest things—
Shells for you to make earrings from or ornaments
For the chests of sea sculptures, your men and women
With the curly green seaweed hair of the truly mad—
An empty bottle for me to puff a song into
Till my eyes fill with a self-made storm of sand.

I should have folded a note inside, written in pictogram
Language: a man and woman by the sea,
Watching the waves go flat while a pelican
Rises from the broken surface with a fish in its beak,
A summer of plenty dispensing. And always a plane
Waiting in a corner of the sky. In that newly cleared zone,
Our outlined figures embraced before your plane took the place of the sun.

LINES IN REGARD TO A MORNING SWIM

Would you not like to leave your hotel
Room where the window looks at the sea?
Would you not find the bathing suit in your valise,

Take a stroll down the carpeted hall, ride the elevator
Six floors to the lobby where the staff is busy
Keeping busy, polishing and wiping every surface,

Including the fronds of the artificial palms?
Would you not like to hear "good mornings"
And "thank yous" and "my pleasures"? Would you not

Answer in the languages you pretend to know
Before passing the eight low-backed stools,
Empty now except for a newspaper and a foaming

Cup on the bar of someone who must be returning?
Huge ceramic vases standing before the revolving door
Look like the queen's guard. What is inside them? No one

Has looked in years: cigarette foil, gum wrappers,
Perhaps a watch battery or a wedding ring, something
One might see when the hotel gets sold for office space,

When the vases are auctioned off and inside is found
A dead mouse. Would you not rather think of something else,
Like the person not your partner you imagine during sex?

Your mouth is dry and you wish you ate or drank
Again this morning before you exited the property
In the white terry robe that you strip and fold on

The sand under your sunglasses, cap, and gel.
Flapping your arms, you walk hip-deep into the sea,
Diving into your shadow, surfacing with no fish in your teeth.

THE MEASUREMENT OF WORDS

The light is so light
I cannot feel it on my shoulders
Even though I am naked
As a sculpture in the park
Of my yard. I ask the sky,
How much does the light weigh?
Is it heavier inside or out of doors?

I hear thunder.
What is the weight of thunder
Or the sound of a voice
When its speaker is gone?
Why like the thunder
Does its meaning increase
Like the silence of a starless night
Or the last breeze of August?

What did August weigh?
Was it more than the notes from a horn
Or the memory of a linen dress
And a figure's absence in the hall?
What is the weight of a color?
Does green cost more than red?
If I could save forever,
Would I buy a bracelet of blue?

LINES OF THE MIRAGE

It takes a desert to realize your mistakes,
The failed mining towns and the mines themselves,

The naked mountains never getting closer,
Illusionary oases awaiting—or if you ever

Found true water amid cottonwoods
And shade, perhaps you would never leave,

Even if it meant you would starve.
I would rather be hungry than thirsty

You said, having eaten your horse and saddle.
Still in the night you build a fire.

AFTER THE EXHIBITION

They came back to the hotel after one of their best days,
Walking around a city they had come to enjoy. It had been
Raining and their clothes were wet and the room was cold
And he raised the heat and shivered naked under the covers
While across the room she charged her phone and texted
Her children. The look in her eyes was always beautiful to him,
And he knew he looked at her too much. She told him so.

Warming, he was waiting for her to get up from the desk
With its electric socket even though there was one next
To the bed. Rising, she said she felt a little sick, then
Sat in the bathroom posting pictures of paintings they saw
At the exhibition at the museum. Before opening the door,
She took one of herself in the mirror. In a few minutes many friends
Liked it and one fellow commented she looked like a "masterpiece."

THE ENCHANTED BELLS

He bought them at the flea market
While she sifted through the *brocante*
For treasures to bring back on the plane
And post on her home page. He noticed
Four bells made of brass without a score
Of provenance or country of origin
(She would later say India when he said Spain)
Etched upon their lips
When he picked them up
Off the vendor's table. Four bells
Arranged separately, perhaps
Haphazardly, amid keys and hand tools,
Pocketknives, medallions, and doorknobs.
All things old and metal, pulled from boxes
Stacked beside a white panel truck.
Four bells with tags of different prices
Dangling from their stems. Four bells
Like Bosc pears fat around their bottoms,
Bought for a price he knew
The vendor would accept.
"For all," he said, for the bells of brass
So cheap he did not even ring them,
Three of which belonged as a set,
The fourth, the smallest, alike in shape
And similar in design but not pattern.
Four bells, the vendor wrapped in newspaper

And wiped the smudges of ink on her apron.
"My woman became lost," he practiced,
Walking back and forth among the tables
Until he saw her with her arms full of bracelets
And her neck adorned with vintage chains.
She was cross with him for having left
Her without a translator for her goods.
Back in the hotel while she bathed,
He tested the timbre of the bells
The vendor had wrapped for him.
The headlines were no better
Than the ones at home. Things just looked
Better for him in another language.
Then he tried the bells, starting large
To small, then back again.
Such bright notes, issuing
Like songbirds from their throats.
He found when he chimed them,
They pealed even rounder, and like
A lookout man he was tempted
To cry out the time in four directions.
When she stepped out of the bathroom,
He thought she was going to tell him
Off again. Instead she dropped
Her towel and kissed him with her tongue.

STORMY TUESDAYS

He remembers stormy Tuesdays that lasted for years
After they parted on a Tuesday, and sometimes even
On a Monday it rains inside him outside a shop
He knows she would like where they sell polka-dot
Sheets and pajamas or golden hair sticks from India,
Some store at the intersection of here-and-there,
Surely more then-than-now because now is nothing
He could bring back as a souvenir she would want
From him, some token dredged from the past,
An artfully labeled bottle of wine, white orchids or
The recollection of dinners in little restaurants
Near coastal waters, the way she broke the crisp
Fish skin with her fork, how with her fingers she took
The last morsels of the cheeks and stripped
The bones and left the flounder looking like
A cartoon comb. Now he cannot see a plate
Without thinking of their time together, or pause
Outside the little shops where once he stood
What seemed like hours in a bad temper,
Where now he waits in the weather for her on a day
That feels like a Tuesday gone bad for him forever.

WINDOW PEEPING INTO THE GARDEN OF EDEN

Like Adam and Eve in the backyard,
My parents on the lawn furniture were
Having at each other on a warm day
On the pads under the cover
Of a high fence that kept out the watching
Eyes of neighbors, but not their son
Cutting school, looking out the kitchen
Window to see her riding him among
The roses and geraniums. I had gone
To the refrigerator and was washing
Blueberries in the sink. After
They pulled on their bathing suits,
I stepped out into the garden. What
Could I do but offer them fruit?

LINES ALONG A WILD PLACE

I walked through the enterprise of weeds.
A crow for each of us stood mounted on a fence.

Sometimes I miss everyone I ever loved
When their faces reflect in the hard, wide

Leaves of the magnolia, their names like blossoms
And their lives once so real and fragrant

Now like handkerchiefs beneath the trees.
If my dog were alive he might piss on them,

And I would have to yell at him not to
If anyone were around.

If anyone were around,
I would say I had momentous news

To tell but forget what it is.
I will ask the dogwoods to remind me

What it means to live along the edges of the woods,
To be promiscuous but bear white flowers.

NOTES, ELEGIAC

"The Work Zone": for James Lester Clark.
"Lines about Emptiness": for Franz Wright.
"Lines along the Shore": for Derek Walcott.
"Lines in the Backyard": for Lucie Brock-Broido.
"For Hubert Desmarest": difficult beloved friend.
"For Oksana Shachko": Ukrainian artist and cofounder of FEMEN.
"Window Peeping into the Garden of Eden": for Linda Gregg.